D0457038

PR
6011
R9
Z82

38260

Stanford
Christopher Fry

CHRISTOPHER FRY

CHRISTOPHER FRY

by

DEREK STANFORD

SOLANO COLLEGE LIBRARY

PUBLISHED FOR
THE BRITISH COUNCIL
BY LONGMAN GROUP LTD

LONGMAN GROUP LTD
Longman House, Burnt Mill, Harlow, Essex

*Associated companies, branches and
representatives throughout the world*

First published 1954
Revised, 1955, 1962, 1971
© Derek Stanford 1962, 1971

Printed in Great Britain by
F. Mildner & Sons, London, EC1

SBN 0 582 01054 3

CONTENTS

PR
6011
R9
Z82
38260

CHRISTOPHER FRY

I. INTRODUCTORY

THE American critic, Lionel Trilling, once remarked, in his book *The Liberal Imagination*, that, in the future, 'people will eventually be unable to say, "They fell in love and married", let alone understand the language of *Romeo and Juliet*, but will, as a matter of course say, "Their libidinal impulses being reciprocal, they activated their individual erotic drives and integrated them within the same frame of reference"'.

We may smile at the fate promised us here, but the parody serves to indicate the direction of our thinking as well as of our speech. And that direction, very broadly speaking, is a deterministic one. At the back of our thoughts, there rests the supposition that men can be studied and known like things; that history is only extended natural history and that nature is reducible to chemistry and physics.

I am not suggesting that all of us find ourselves happy with these notions. They are dogmas and hypotheses we have absorbed during the course of our lives. Nor is the exact degree of our intellectual assent to them the really cardinal factor in the influence they exert. The climate of ideas in which we exist is largely fashioned by such theories. We inherit and imbibe them in every situation, and their constant presence comes to be felt, by the most imaginative and aspiring, as an obstacle to a more generous and expansive mode of thinking and living. And that which a few consciously recognize, a great many others are dimly aware of.

It is by a reaction from this point of view that I would explain the all-round success of Fry's plays. In a universe often viewed as mechanistic, he has posited the principle of mystery: in an age of necessitarian ethics, he has stood unequivocally for ideas of free-will. In theatre technique, he has gaily ignored the sacrosanct conventions of natural-

istic drama; and in terms of speech, he has brought back
poetry on to the stage with undoctored abandon.

We may ask if the satisfaction of these needs should lead
us to reckon Fry as a prophet, but before answering we
should recall that a prophet is describable as one with a
message, as one who proclaims that message with an often
narrow single-minded aim. Now this definition will not
hold for Fry. The powerful vision of existence he possesses
is broad and diffused, and cannot be reduced to one imper-
ative command or formula. We touch upon it here and
there in the plays; as when, in *A Sleep of Prisoners*, man's
life on earth is spoken of as 'an obstinate anticipation of
love'; when Moses, in *The Firstborn*, sums up the conflict
between freedom and predestination with the words:

> I do not know why the necessity of God
> Should feed on grief but it seems so;

when Thomas Mendip, in *The Lady's Not for Burning*, for
all his misanthropy, admits that 'something condones the
world incorrigibly', and counsels Jennet Jourdemayne, the
rational-minded 'witch', to 'Rest in the riddle' of existence;
or, again, when in the same play, he laughs at Jennet's
scientific preconceptions:

> We have given you a world as contradictory
> As a female, as cabbalistic as the male,
> A conscienceless hermaphrodite who plays
> Heaven off against hell, hell off against heaven,
> Revolving in the ballroom of the skies
> Glittering with conflict as with diamonds:
> We have wasted paradox and mystery on you
> When all you ask for, is cause and effect!
> A copy of your birth-certificate was all you needed
> To make you at peace with Creation. How uneconomical
> The whole thing's been.

We sense the import of this vision in Dynamene's phrase
in *A Phoenix Too Frequent*, 'Love is the only discipline'; in

Tappercoom's statement, in *The Lady's Not for Burning*:

> Religion
> Has made an honest woman of the supernatural
> And we won't have it kicking over the traces again;

In Cymen's question, in *Thor, with Angels*:

> By what stroke was the human flesh
> Hacked so separate from the body of life;

and once more, in his exclamation to the gods:

> You make us to be the eternal alien
> In our own world;

in the grim wisdom of Tegeus, in *A Phoenix Too Frequent*:

> I should have known:
> Indulgences, not fulfilment, is what the world
> Permits us;

in Perpetua's statement of belief, in *Venus Observed*, that 'everyone's heart is a great eccentric'; or in Thomas's remark, in *The Lady's Not for Burning*, that laughter is

> an irrelevancy
> Which almost amounts to revelation

(for the metaphysical, the mystical, and the comic are intimately related in Fry); or, in the confession of the Chorus in *The Boy with a Cart*:

> Coming out from our doorways on October nights
> We have seen the sky unfreeze and a star drip
> Into the south: *experienced alteration*
> *Beyond experience.*[1]

But the meaning of Fry's vision comes to a head in many places, according to the situations of the play.

As I have suggested, his success is to be looked for not in any single manifestation, but in a combination of quali-

[1] The italics are mine.

ties, each of which satisfied a need in his audience: the need
for mystery, the need for fantasy, the need for language of
a richer fuller consistency than the 'processed' daily speech
the London stage afforded.

Fry's verbal contribution I would like to describe by the
word 'immediacy'; and it is an antidote to the absence
of this element in pre-war drama that he owes much of his
reputation. For before the arrival of Fry as a playwright, the
English stage—regarded as something more than a mere
arena of entertainment—offered two opposed alternatives:[1]
the slick but wooden and short-breathed dialogue of the
naturalistic school; and the heavier, reflective, and literary
syntax of the poetic drama.

But immediacy in Fry is not just a verbal matter: it is
not a question of fluency alone, or of a swift and nimble
identification in terms of language with the objects of the
world. Informing this literary tactile sense in Fry, there exists
a note or 'resonance' of wonder; and 'wonder', writes
Kierkegaard, 'is the sense immediacy has of God and is the
beginning of all deeper understanding'.

Perhaps I can indicate the liberation and scope of Fry's
work, for our present age, by resorting to a distinction
which the Danish philosopher once made. 'For the task
of becoming', he observed, 'possibility and necessity are
equally essential. Just as infinitude and finitude . . . both
belong to the self, so also possibility and necessity. A self
which has no possibility is in despair, and so in turn is the
self which has no necessity.'

During the period between the Wars, literature tended
to view the life of man too often in exclusive antithetical
fashion: either as subject to necessity alone, or as a field of
boundless possibility. Influenced by the theories of Marx

---

[1] The case of Charles Williams is an exception. Plays by him, produced
between 1930 and 1950, combine the vernacular and the poetic in a way
that partly anticipates Fry. But the general restriction of their themes to
traditional religious subject-matter, and their performance on small amateur
stages, accounts for their comparative lack of influence in those years. Their
impact now is being felt more widely.

and Freud, the social and psychological authors saw man as a predetermined creature, starved of the oxygen of chance. In polar contrast to this perspective, the Surrealists, with their theory of 'free association', viewed the human person as a being without boundaries. According to them, the notion of 'hazard' offered a free-pass to futurity. Man was the prince of the present, and the heir of time-to-come instead of being the bond-slave of the past. But if humanity be seen as a ship, the vessel which the Surrealists envisaged was unseaworthy through lack of ballast. Licence is a form of enslavement just as certainly as necessity.

Both these artistic attitudes history and personal experience prove wrong. But, for the main part, contemporary literature has erred by accenting necessity.

Fry has relieved us from the pressure of both of these dilemmas, because in his work the sense of possibility and necessity are well balanced. For example, the Duke in *Venus Observed* has realized, by the end of the play, that his days of amorous adventuring are over. His sturdy middle age is approaching its decline, and boasts of youthful prowess no longer apply. 'Shall I be sorry for myself?' he asks. 'In mortality's name I'll be sorry for myself.' But from this knowledge of limitation, he decides to snatch a victory. Necessity has become a virtue, because it has shown him the limits of his powers. It has made clear to him that he can no longer expect to capture and collect the hearts of the young; and because the endless possibilities of philandering have been removed from him, he learns to know his proper need. Resolving to marry an older woman, whose actions have helped to bring about his present state of painful self-knowledge, he decides that old age is itself an adventure. 'Shall I be happy for myself?' he queries. 'In the name of existence I'll be happy for myself'; and goes on to imagine his future in terms of the attractions of the autumn landscape.

In these passages we are given the systole and diastole of human aspiration and its concomitant limitation. Necessity and possibility are displayed as opposites, but they are shown as inter-acting, each in their turn giving rise to the other.

But both the necessity and the possibility currently assumed to control human life, especially in its representation on the stage, are repudiated by Fry as offering only a very inadequate account of our condition. Considering the causes for 'the flight of poetry from the theatre' between the Jacobean and the Restoration era, Fry remarks[1] how 'the accent of living changed from the adventuring soul to the body's welfare. God was changed from being as it were a magnet attracting the steel of the spirit, to the absentee boss of a welfare state. It happened almost in a night. When the sun rose in the morning it was no longer Apollo but Mammon. . . . In the brave new world, the Restoration theatre, the spirit becomes *esprit*, and as such did very well. But we have only to compare two comedies of a similar order, *Love's Labour's Lost* and *The Way of the World*, and we see what has gone; instinctive apprehension of our nature, apprehending and apprehensive in the modern sense; we have gained verisimilitude but we have lost truth.'

II. BIOGRAPHICAL

Christopher Fry was born at Bristol, in the West Country, in 1907. His parents' home was a small, single-fronted, unimposing one; and home-life, though comfortable, was far from being luxurious.

His father had begun his career as a building contractor, and found his business anything but thriving. Just when his difficult uphill struggle appeared to be taking a better turn, he decided to abandon his profession and give himself up to work for the poor. In those days, Bristol had its share of poverty; and Fry's father, as an Anglican lay-preacher, found his parish in the city slums. Often, after being out all day,

[1] In an article 'Poetry and the Theatre', contributed to the bilingual review *Adam* (Year XIX, nos. 214-15, 1951).

he would return to carry off his supper to some sick or destitute person. His zeal was immense, but the affliction he encountered preyed upon him; and in 1910, his health shattered, he died a martyr to his mission.

Fry, who was only three at his death, retained deep and powerful impressions of his father. The faith and personality of his parent had always meant much to him, and constituted a kind of subconscious ideal. It is possible that these filial emotions are reflected in his early work *The Boy with a Cart*, for the father of the future St Cuthman (the hero of the play) dies when the boy is still young, and his son's words upon him paint a vivid tender portrait. Possible, too, is the relationship between the missionary urgency of certain of Fry's compositions (*The Firstborn*, *Thor, with Angels*, and *A Sleep of Prisoners*) and his father's example.

Fry's mother was also a religious-minded woman. Although Church of England herself, she came of Quaker stock; and Fry, who sent his son to a Quaker public school, has something of the Quaker about him to this day. Indeed, it is probably the unusual combination of an early theatrical background with inherited Quaker tendencies that constitute the distinctness of his temperament: a nature both grave and gay, contemplative and sociable; and, above all, enamoured of quiet and peace.

Also important in Fry's upbringing were an aunt and a teacher, both religious women, one of whom early inspired him with a love of English literature by reading the prose of Bunyan to him.

In spite of straitened circumstances, Fry was given a good education at the Bedford Modern School, one of the best foundations of its kind. Here he remained until he was eighteen, after which he tried his hand at teaching for about a year.

But the theatre was quick to claim him. Already, at school, he had written his second play (his first play, at the age of fourteen, being an unacted and unpublished verse-drama), *Youth and The Peregrines*, which was performed in 1934, and earlier still had taken part in civic and kindergarten pageants. For a while he joined a repertory company, only to be driven back, by the precariousness of stage living, to a second round of teaching. His publishers refer to this as 'a brief reactionary interlude'; and there can be little doubt that Fry is one, like Hamlet, born both to find and teach the truth by 'indirection' rather than 'direction'. After he had saved the sum of £10, he left the environment of teaching for good; and from 1934 to 1936 acted as director for the Tunbridge Wells Repertory Players. In the latter year Fry was married to the journalist, Phyllis Hart, obtaining by his marriage a centre of security in a career quite often insecure.

Unlike most poetic dramatists, Fry is firstly a man of the theatre. His training-ground has been the stage rather than the library or the study; and it is this first-hand experience of the medium he writes for that helps to give him his immediacy of expression.

On quitting teaching for a second time, Fry became what fifty years back might have been termed 'a strolling player'. During those days he acted as a kind of theatrical jack-of-all-trades, putting himself to any task provided it had connexions with the stage. One of these jobs was as secretary to a popular song-hit writer. Fry, who plays the piano by ear, always had a musical nature; and in 1935 a musical-comedy by him, with the title of *She Shall Have Music*, enjoyed a brief run at the Savoy Theatre.[1] This interest still prevails; and in 1951 he composed the music, which Leslie Bridgewater scored for him, for Peter Brooks's production of Shakespeare's *A Winter's Tale*. This was followed in 1953 by the extra lyrics he wrote for the film of John Gay's *The Beggar's Opera*.

After a spell of song-writing, Fry worked for a while as a cabaret entertainer; and in 1934 he joined the Repertory Players at Tunbridge Wells. Here he both acted and directed, playing the principal male lead in the *première* of Bernard

[1] Save where otherwise stated, all theatres mentioned in this essay are in London.

Shaw's *A Village Wooing* (which he had secured for his Company).

Up to 1939, although he had written one or two plays that had been put on at rather special, and sometimes limited occasions, Fry had had none of his dramas published. He had, for example, under commission, written a piece which dramatized the life of the founder of Dr Barnardo's Homes, with the title of *Open Door*. Other productions, staged but not published, were *The Tower* (1939), a work written for the Tewkesbury Festival, showing the influence of Eliot's pageant *The Rock*, and another pageant of similar nature entitled *Thursday's Child*, which was performed at the Albert Hall in the same year. He also contributed a number of playlets for the Children's service of the BBC.

Many of these facts are more important as showing Fry's comprehensive stage background than as theatrical features or activities in their own right. Their true significance lies in enabling us to understand that between this poet and the theatre there was none of that apologetic patronizing aloofness with which the literary author so often approaches the stage. Fry's hand was dyed to the colour of the boards.

In 1937 came the festival play *The Boy with a Cart*, which served to introduce Fry to the Religious Drama Society and its President, the Bishop of Chichester. The text of the play was published in 1939; and is, accordingly, the first of Fry's work to assume permanent form.

In 1940 he became director of the Oxford Playhouse, a few months before his call-up. After serving for four years in a non-combatant arm of the Forces, he returned to the Oxford Playhouse, and the completion of his tragedy *The Firstborn*, which he had been writing when war overtook him. The text of the play was published in 1946, and in the same year there came the first of his comedies, *A Phoenix Too Frequent*. Presented at the Mercury Theatre, and later revived at the Arts Theatre, the play captured both the public and the critics. This was followed in 1948 by a second comedy, *The Lady's Not for Burning*, produced initially at the

Arts Theatre, and going next year to The Globe under the direction of John Gielgud. *The Lady* was an even greater success with London theatre-goers; and in 1950 there came a third comedy, *Venus Observed*, directed by Sir Laurence Olivier and performed at St James's Theatre. The same year saw also Fry's version of Jean Anouilh's *L'Invitation au Château* (under the title of *Ring Round the Moon*), and a further religious play, *Thor, with Angels*.

In 1951, as part of the programme for the Festival of Britain, Fry wrote his third religious play, *A Sleep of Prisoners*, which was first performed in St Mary's, Oxford, church of the 'silver-tongued' Newman.

In 1952, his tragedy *The Firstborn* was given its London début, after having been acted in 1948 at the Edinburgh Festival. He was now a playwright of international reputation.

As a man, Fry is modest and home-loving. He prefers the country to the town, and thinks that authors should imitate painters and try composing in the open air. In appearance, he is short but well-built; dark and good-looking in a way that almost suggests Spanish blood. In speech, he is a little slow and low-spoken; and his glance and voice are measured and reflective.

III. THE PLAYS

Fry's published dramas are ten[1] in number: three 'religious festival' plays [*The Boy with a Cart* (1939),[2] *Thor, with Angels* (1950), and *A Sleep of Prisoners* (1951)]; five comedies [*A Phoenix Too Frequent* (1946), *The Lady's Not for Burning* (1949), *Venus Observed* (1950), *The Dark is Light Enough* (1954), and *A Yard of Sun* (1970)]; a tragedy [*The Firstborn* (1946)], and a history play *Curtmantle* (1961).

About these works there is a remarkable unity. All of them, according to their genre, are concerned in the words of Private Meadows in *A Sleep of Prisoners*, with an 'explor-

[1] Plus six translations, which I consider on pages 39–43.
[2] The dates given are those of publication, not performance.

ation into God'. They all, directly or indirectly, ask what the nature of our existence is, in which predicament so plentifully flowers. Sometimes they envisage the mortal dilemma as a mysterious case for mirth, and sometimes as a cause for weeping; and always as something which has its spring, its resolution and understanding in God.

Neither are the categories in which Fry writes his plays closed watertight compartments of tragic or comic expression. There are many humorous incidents and speeches in the religious pieces; while the comedies are all nearly tragic in their upshot. The death of a husband, and the presence of malefactors' corpses, marks *A Phoenix Too Frequent*, in addition to which the hero of the play barely escapes capital punishment. In *The Lady's Not for Burning* the heroine is sentenced to the stake, and is pardoned unofficially at the last moment. The third comedy, *Venus Observed*, presents us with an act of arson, by which the two chief characters are almost destroyed in a blazing observatory. 'So much I delighted in is all of ash', reflects the protagonist after the fire. Finally, *The Dark is Light Enough* ends with the death of the Countess Rosmarin as the Austrian soldiery hammer on the door of her country house. Such are the grim macabre trappings to a set of comedies whose lines have made their audience laugh and laugh again. Even the more elevated and single-minded tragedy *The Firstborn* is rich in humour of a mordant order. In the words of Doto in *A Phoenix Too Frequent*, Fry realizes that

life and death
Is cat and dog in this double-bed of a world.

'Progress', writes Fry in a note of dedication to *A Sleep of Prisoners*, 'is the growth of vision: the increased perception of what makes for life and what makes for death', and he goes on to state how he has sought 'to find a way for comedy to say something of this'.

When we read Fry's comedies, then, we must be prepared to discover in them a meaning as deep and permanent as we tend to look for, these days, in tragedy. And likewise, when we read the religious plays, we must not take the laughter to be out of place nor deem it a mark of unthinking irreverence.

(a) *The Festival Plays*

Each of these three pieces, like Fry's other drama, has a manifest and latent theme or content. On the surface, *The Boy with a Cart* is the story of how the Cornish St Cuthman came to found the church of Steyning in Sussex: at a deeper level, the play presents us with the struggle between faith and convention. Similarly, *Thor, with Angels*, tells how a Jutish household in Kent was converted to Christianity by St Augustine of Canterbury's mission, while on another plane it shows us the debate between self-assertion and self-transcendence, the way of exploitation and the way of compassion. Thirdly, in *A Sleep of Prisoners*, we follow the moods of four soldiers, imprisoned in an enemy church in wartime. The play seems to be about their respective prejudices and antipathies, nervously intensified by their confinement, but at the same time depicts a conflict between the loving open mind and the closed view of life which sees hate as necessary —an argument between the claims of war and peace.

Notwithstanding this 'double-level' appeal, these pieces are not to be considered as 'moralities' or allegories. The characters are not conceived as abstracts of the vices and virtues, but as individual beings. The feeling we have that these characters, and their situations, stand for something beyond themselves, is an impression all deep art communicates.

The Boy with a Cart is a bucolic play. The account of how a young shepherd, whose father has died, constructs a wooden cart in which he carries his mother about with him until they come to the village of Steyning, where, in face of obstacles, he builds a church, does not bother itself with a plot. Apart from a couple of miracles (light-hearted examples of divine intervention), the incidents are homely and the characters simple.

The chorus of 'The People of South England' in this play shows the influence of T. S. Eliot's *Murder in the Cathedral*:

> Out of this, out of the first incision
> Of mortality on mortality, there comes
> The genuflexion, and the partition of pain
> Between man and God; there grows the mutual action,
> The perspective to the vision.

In Fry's later plays, this influence (towards a poetry of abstract nouns) is absent. A second influence, however, and one which Fry has continued to develop, is that of Charles Williams. Compare, for likeness, the following lines from Fry's chorus:

> In our fields, fallow and burdened, in grass and furrow
> In barn and stable, with scythe, flail, or harrow,
> Sheepshearing, milking or mowing, on labour that's older
> Than knowledge, with God we work shoulder to shoulder;
> God providing, we dividing, sowing, and pruning;
> Not knowing yet and yet sometimes discerning

with Charles Williams's lines from his play *Seed of Adam*:[1]

> Dullards of darkness, light's lazybones,
> poor primitives of our natural bareness,
> where's your awareness? will moans and groans
> for gold or brawn or brain regain
> the way to the entry of Paradise? up!

In both of these passages there is a use of internal rhyme and of studied controlled alliteration; and further lines from *Thor, with Angels* show how Fry has retained and intensified his use of these devices:

> Nullify guilt and mollify the gods
> And bury the brat's guts for good in the ground.

[1] *Seed of Adam* was first produced in 1936, and published in 1937 in the magazine *Christendom*. *The Boy with a Cart* was first produced in 1937, and published in 1939.

Already, in this play we begin to notice the breaking buds of Fry's verbal flowering. 'We have seen', recite the chorus, 'old women dandling shadows'—a reference to the children they carried in their arms when they were young, the memory of which is still with them. In the same abbreviated way, the cessation of farmwork at evening is suggested by the line:

> The darkness hangs the hatchet in the barn.

Some of the speeches of this play are written in prose, but the same condensed vision informs their imagery. Looking back at 'the sun on the white walls' of the village in which he was born, and which he will never revisit, Cuthman describes the walls as 'my swaddling clothes put out to dry. I am out of them once and for all.'

In these three examples, we have the first workings of that cryptic and oblique mode of expression which tells us so much more than a literal statement, and which Fry has gone on to develop ever since.

Thor, with Angels is a more ambitious work. The characters are more numerous and fully drawn; and the action more dramatic and symbolic. The thought and poetry are richer and deeper; and the humour and pathos excellently balanced.

Cymen, a Jutish freebooter, returns from battle against the Saxons. He and his men had been carrying the field, when their onrush was halted by a young British slave fighting on the Saxon side. He had already killed one of their chief warriors, and was hemmed in by Jutish spears, when Cymen leapt to his rescue, straddled his fallen body, and broke his own sword over his head.

His gesture amazes everybody, not least Cymen himself (who swears that his sword was broken by a 'blinding light'). Wishing to know more about this unseen force that has suddenly entered his life, Cymen takes the young Briton prisoner, feeling, in an obscure way, that there is some strange relationship between him and the hidden power.

Cymen and his followers return to their homestead, taking the Briton with them. There the young prisoner meets Merlin, too old and near-sighted now

> To be able to distinguish one thing from another,
> The storm-swollen river from the tear-swollen eyes
> Or the bare cracked earth from the burnt-out face,
> Or the forest soughing from the sighing heart.

Cymen learns that before the Briton had been captured by the Saxons he had been baptized a Christian, though the details of his faith have grown dim in his mind. The Jute would like to sacrifice the prisoner in order to placate his own violent gods, but is withheld by the same unlocated power when he makes to do so. Summoned by a messenger to a general assembly, there—at the command of the King of Kent—

> To receive the person and words of Augustine
> Exponent of the Christian God—

Cymen departs, instructing his family that the Briton is not to be killed in his absence. His warning is ignored, however; and on the excuse that the Briton is trying to seduce Cymen's daughter, they drag him to a tree and spear him, just as Cymen returns home converted. Faith and sacrifice have come together.

The character of Merlin in this play serves as an intermediary between the thought of the pagan Jutes and the Christians whose second coming he prophesies. His words are wise and mellow, and saturate with poetry; but his most important speech of sixty-odd lines is probably too lengthy in its dramatic context. This speech (beginning with the words 'Welcome, sleep . . .') should be carefully studied by readers of Fry. In it, he appears to interpret human life somewhat in the terms of the philosophy of 'emergent evolution'. As I have elsewhere[1] shown, it is also possible to

---

[1] *Christopher Fry—An Appreciation* (1951).

find in his speech a poetic transcription of certain of the ideas of Plato and Aristotle. It must always be remembered, though, that Fry is no systematic thinker; and the evidence or presence of ideas in this speech should not necessarily be taken as applying to his thoughts in other contexts.

Fry—whose principal characters are all 'Everyman in his Humour'—sometimes succeeds and sometimes fails in creating specifically humorous types. Colgrin, the lazy serving-man in this play—

> (It doesn't do a man any good, daylight.
> It means up and doing, and that means up to no good.
> The best life is led horizontal . . .)—

is, like Doto in *A Phoenix Too Frequent*, clearly a triumph, just as Reddleman and Bates in *Venus Observed* are examples of the ready-made 'cut-out' clown.

A Sleep of Prisoners might be described as a Passion Play, in which man endures the crucifixion of history. And if it be asked what are the forces behind this crucifying process, Fry's answer would seem to be that they are prejudice, intolerance, and hatred. But if man is subjected to history's crucifixion, unlike Christ he does not purchase the gift of redemption with his pain. Salvation follows sacrifice, only if the sacrifice is offered in love.

So it comes about that the sacrifices which men endure in wars (those 'cures' we use 'which never cure') are ineffective in obtaining lasting peace. Unless one can 'learn to forgive [the] necessity' by which one is confronted, that necessity is one's doom. Only a necessity (in the form of an enemy, say) which we succeed in approaching with love can ever act upon us to our salvation. In the broadest sense of the term, *A Sleep of Prisoners* is a pacifist play.

It is also experimental in construction. In it, Fry has welded contemporary experience and Biblical material into one dramatic whole, from which he elicits certain truths of conduct. This integration is achieved by means of a dream technique: the characters sleep, and in their sleep become identified with Bible figures whose natures or situations have cogent bearing on their own. Through their dream-identification, they discover more about themselves, more about their friends, and something too about the general predicament of man.

The dreams that lead to this self-discovery embody incidents of great significance: Cain's murder of Abel; Joab's assassination of Absalom at the command of King David; Abraham's near-sacrifice of his son Isaac; and the experience of the three men (Shadrach, Meshach, and Abed-nego) in the fiery furnace.

The pace and tension of this play is tremendous, and the language has a furious urgency about it. Fry's severest critics, who pronounce his work to be deficient in action, could not sustain the charge in this instance. *A Sleep of Prisoners* is a drama full of the naked friction of wills; their impact, conflict, and explosion. It is 'theatre' in the most physical sense. And yet, with all these points in its favour, I feel that this play—with its powerful and ingenious structure—is a little too ingenious in its ending. A drama, packed with terror and pity, is curiously converted at its close to a noble-minded oration. Argument replaces catastrophe; and we are the poorer, though the happier, for it.

(b) *The Comedies*

Fry's chief contribution to the genre of dramatic constructions is the *Comedy of Seasons*—a statement to be taken both literally and metaphorically. Literally, because the category is one of his own devising; and metaphorically, because he has put his theory into practice and given us plays based on this idea.

Venus Observed, the dramatist has told us, 'was planned as one of a series of four comedies, a comedy for each of the seasons of the year, four comedies of mood'.[1] 'I don't know whether', he continues, 'a comedy of mood is an

---

[1] See his article '*Venus* Considered' in *Theatre Newsletter*, 11 March 1950.

accepted category, or whether it's something I've coined to cover my particular end. It means that the scene, the season, and the characters, are bound together in one climate. In *Venus* the season is autumn, the scene is a house beginning to fall into decay, the characters, most of them, are in middle life.'[1]

The same idea of seasonal influence, which Fry has perfected in *Venus Observed*, is also present in *The Lady's Not for Burning*. 'I have tried',[2] he has written of this play, 'to make the words and the deeds of the characters move all the time with a sense of the particular moment at which they are said or done, so that we can be aware continually of the April afternoon, for example, with the scents and sounds of it, or of the April evening and night as the play goes on: moreover, to make these scents and sounds an essential part of the action, conditioning the words of the characters. For instance, Thomas Mendip in Act II stands at the window watching and describing to Jennet the dusk which has descended on the Cotswolds, and his treatment of her in the ensuing scene is conditioned by that, leading him to rally her with such lines as:

> This evening is a ridiculous wisp of down
> Blowing in the air as disconsolately as dust.

leading him, indeed, eventually to a perplexity of his own, to the discovery that, although he finds life intolerable, yet "Something condones the world, incorrigibly".

Fry disclaims any originality for this harmonic notion of dramatic treatment, but admits that 'the use of it in recent years has not been frequent'. From the viewpoint of contemporary realism, he agrees 'it is easy enough to see no connexion between a lyrical passage about the dusk and the action that follows it', but defends his manner of working mainly on two grounds. The first of these refers to a unify-

[1] Ibid.
[2] See his article '*The Lady's Not for Burning*' in *World Review*, June 1949.

ing intuition of the world, and the second to a mode of expression which follows naturally from it. 'Nothing', writes Fry, 'is absolutely itself; everything carries with it a proportion of its neighbourhood.' And then, posed with the question of why he 'uses poetry instead of prose', he replies: 'Well, if we have to be born into a world so wildly unprosaic as this one is, what else can be done, if we mean to be realistic.'

Related to *The Lady's Not for Burning* and *Venus Observed* by reason of its vivid imagery, its lyricism and gaiety of spirit—but not intended as *a comedy of seasons*—is Fry's play *A Phoenix Too Frequent*. The story of the play is based on Petronius's tale of the Ephesian matron, who determined to starve herself to death in her husband's tomb, was led to change her mind on the appearance of a blithe young corporal of the guard. What Fry satirizes in this play is not a romantic conception of love (as a union consisting of more than animal lust), but the false heroics of a sentimental ideal. The self-immolation of widows (however Hindus may regard it) is an unreal gesture for the European. 'Oh, how the inveterate body,' exclaims Dynamene, the widow in this play,

> Even when cut from the heart, insists on leaf
> Puts out, with a meaningless separate will,
> Fronds to intercept the thankless sun.
> How it does, oh, how it does.

Throughout this play we are aware of the powers of the summer night subtly working upon Dynamene, in order to win her back to life from the false position of her suicidal love. And, potently aided by the corporal, the forces of life finally prevail. Yet when her new lover calls her to his arms, her speech does not give us the impression that Dynamene's desire is solely physical. Indeed, it refines on the idea of love in the very moment of physical embracing:

> I am there before I reach you; my body
> Only follows to join my longing which

> Is holding you already.—Now I am
> All one again.

In the speech of Dynamene which follows this, we detect the tone of animal appetite; yet other needs are vocal within it so that—frank and direct as it is—we cannot maintain that it represents the language of simple sexual hunger:

>   O all
> In myself; it covets all in you,
> My care, my Chromis. Then I shall be
> Creation.

Here we have a woman saying that she wants affection, embraces, and a child. All three related needs we tend today to distinguish and separate; but Fry treats them as a unity, with the result that his statement is at the same time primitive and complex. What he so singularly preserves in his language is the sense of mystery in primal matters. For him, flesh is not the antithesis of spirit; for mystery is the breath of spirit, and spirit the prime mover of the flesh. And the mystery is also extremely humorous: a paradox of uproarious implications.

Fry describes how he set out to write *The Lady's Not for Burning*, envisaging it as the 'first cousin to an artificial comedy'.[1] 'I could see no reason,' he goes on to say, 'though writing such a comedy, why I should not treat the world as I see it, a world in which we are all poised on the edge of eternity, a world which has deeps and shadows of mystery, in which God is anything but a sleeping partner.' An artificial comedy with a difference, indeed!

The theme of *The Lady's Not for Burning* is misanthropy converted to acceptance by love, and rationalism converted to a sense of the mystery of existence by just the same factor. Thomas Mendip (a fourteenth-century captain-adventurer) is a curious mixture of Hamlet and Prometheus. Unable to find a meaning in life, he gives himself up as a murderer

---

[1] See the article *'The Lady's Not for Burning'* in *World Review*, June 1949.

(when, in fact, no murder has been committed), and insists on being hanged. Not until the young rationalist-minded daughter of an alchemist is convicted as a witch and sentenced to be burnt does he consent to live, in the hope of contriving her escape.

Fry, in a foreword to the first edition, has suggested that we might think of this play 'in terms of light, of inconstant April sunshine, of sunset, twilight, and full moon; of human intelligence in a dance together, sometimes with nothing but buoyancy, sometimes with a seriousness which has been sufficiently mocked by distress to be able to mock back'. April, in this play, is a cruel and beautiful month,¹ but unlike the springtime of Eliot's *Four Quartets*, the springtide that we meet here is still in 'time's covenant'.

As always in Fry's plays, love necessitates or is accompanied by some mode or other of death; but in the comedies there follows resurrection. Fry's optimism, 'mocked by distress', knows how 'to mock back'.

Venus Observed tells the story of a middle-ageing amorist, who seeks in the thought of marriage the only possible escape from affairs-without-end. But his philandering has reached such a point that he no longer trusts himself to choose. He therefore appoints his son to perform the act of selection for him; about the future result of which he expresses himself with bland indifference:

> Shall I be happy on Tuesdays, Thursdays, and Saturdays,
> Or on Mondays, Wednesdays, and Fridays? Some such
>   difference
> Is all that your choice involves.

But a fresh alternative arrives, who is both young and beautiful. Father and son contend for her; and, at length, age retires before youth, resolved to discover in 'an ancient love', 'like summer / Visiting St Martin', matrimonial peace with the most attached of his past mistresses.

¹ See the first line of *The Waste Land*, by T. S. Eliot.

In this play Fry develops to perfection the idea of a
comedy of seasonal mood. Every page of the text breathes
a proof of autumn: the old, decaying, ducal house; the
eclipse of the sun and the Hallowe'en scenes; the presence
of the Duke's former sweethearts, still attractive, but past
their hey-day; and the handsome Duke, with his own
abating virility, and the fear of a possible lonely old age.
Ripeness poised on the turn to decadence is the informing
spirit of this drama, providing, so to speak, a central cyno-
sure. As the Duke humorously puts it:

> 'Mellow'
> Is the keynote of the hour. We must be mellow,
> Remembering we've been on the earth two million years,
> Man and boy and Sterkfontein ape.

As an example of the inter-revelation which landscape
and spirit afford each other in this play. I will quote one
or two short passages. 'For years', claims the Duke, with
mock self-pity,

> the frost has lain
> On my stubble beard. The swallows and other such
> Migratory birds have left me long ago.

Now this 'ties up' and is 'in tune' with the Duke's description of the scene from the window; but it is not a
business of returning the compliment, as it were. (Pre-
viously, it was the landscape that illuminated the Duke: now
it is the Duke who illustrates the landscape.) When he speaks
of the 'swallows' and other 'migratory birds', he is referring
to the fact that women no longer make so much of him. The
swallow is proverbially the bird of love, and the 'other
migratory birds' may be thought to refer to his light-of-
love affairs. So, decorative though they appear, the terms
of the Duke's figure are to be seen as psychologically
functional.

Similarly, when the Duke, coaching the beautiful young
Perpetua in archery, tells her that

Daylight is short, and becoming always shorter.
But there's the space for an arrow or two between
Now and the sunset

he is speaking as much about the brief years left to him in
the role of a lover, as about the suitable conditions of visi-
bility for their toxophilic exercises; and in Perpetua's reply
we get an example of that half-conscious innocent *double-
entendre* which Fry manages so well, and which is a vehicle
for both humour and poetry:

I've never handled a bow.
How shall I manage?

Here we feel that the heroine is hinting at her inexperience
of men, and at her own virginity. The Duke assures her that
all will be well if she does what he tells her, and Perpetua
promises with the word 'Implicitly'. The whole scene (one
well-sustained metaphor) almost suggests the opening stages
of some ceremony of initiation (heightened by the place in
which it occurs—'The Temple of Ancient Virtue', in which
it was the wont of the third Duchess of Altair to inform her
husband of her pregnancies: twenty-seven in all!)

The character-drawing in *Venus Observed* is fuller and
more reasoned than in the other comedies. Fry has gone in
each case to the motive element behind the personality, and
describes his analysis in the following manner. 'Every other
natural form of life', he writes, 'has a completeness, but in
every human relationship, even the most perfect, there is a
space of the heart, or the mind, unsatisfied, and through this
space men are always reaching towards something which
will complete them. The Duke had always hoped to find it
in sexual love. . . . Reedbeck, the Duke's agent, wages war
against the gap by a passionate longing for the nobility and
leisured civilization that is passing away from the earth, and
is quite conscienceless in the way he tries to attain it. . . . The
butler, Reddleman, has filled the restless space in himself by
the heroic method of lion taming, but he lost his nerve in

the war, has had to leave his lions, and so, lost again himself,
vents his spleen on the footman. The footman has been a
burglar; he had a "pathological lust for climbing ladders,
and had to rationalize it when he got to the top".[1]

Save for his two stock humorous characters—the Cock-
ney footman and the bombastic Irish butler (both over-
written parts)—the people in this play have a real life of
their own. The ladies of the Duke's past: Rosabel, the sensitive, inflammable actress; Hilda, the country type, ironic and
resigned; and Jessie, a kind of regal barmaid, serene, self-
knowing and forgiving,[2] are well suggested. Perpetua,
fresh and eager, too young still to know her own mind;
Dominic, her troubled brother, with his nice undergraduate
conscience; Edgar, the Duke's son, waking himself out
of a boyhood dream of riding and horses; and the dishonest,
delightful Reedbeck, only wanting to have his aphorisms
brightly received by a seemly company: all these form an
impressive and amusing portrait gallery for the cast of one
play.

In Fry's comedies of the seasons, Winter is represented by
his latest play *The Dark is Light Enough*. The dramatist has
chosen as an epigraph to this work a passage from the
naturalist J. H. Fabre:

The weather was stormy; the sky heavily clouded; the darkness . . .
profound. . . . It was across this maze of leafage, and in absolute darkness,
that the butterflies had to find their way in order to attain the end of
their pilgrimage.

Under such conditions the screech-owl would not dare to forsake
its olive-tree. The butterfly . . . goes forward without hesitation. . . .
So well it directs its tortuous flight that, in spite of all the obstacles to
be evaded, it arrives in a state of perfect freshness, its great wings
intact. . . . The darkness is light enough. . . .

[1] See his article '*Venus* Considered' in *Theatre Newsletter*, 11 March 1950.

[2] Or is she a little too kind to be true? Unless we imagine her to be of
comfortable proportions, or see her played by an actress of mature and
ample build, I feel we may find it difficult to encompass the idea of her
wide and easy charity.

It is probable that Fry was bearing in mind the character of his heroine Countess Rosmarin, when he selected this quotation. A grand lady, with a high familiar air, who religiously holds her *soirées* every Thursday, even when the dangers of war intervene and her own death is imminent, the Countess is one who—in George Fox's words—is 'still and cool in her own mind and spirit', however much events may bluster about her. Greeting her friends at her last gathering, when she is mortally ill, she insists on the graces of discourse as usual:

> We must value this evening as the one
> Thursday in the universe, for the rest
> Have gone, and no more may come,
> And we should be on our most immortal behaviour.

But at the back of her cult of courtesy, informing her devotion to humane politeness with something more substantial than a notion of good manners, there dwells an eschatological vision:

> The argument, philosophy, wit and eloquence
> Were all in the light of this end we come to.
> Without it there would have been very little
> To mention except the weather. Protect me
> From a body without death.

The drama of *The Dark is Light Enough* centres round an imaginary incident, which takes place in the Hungarian revolution against the Austro-Hungarian Empire in 1848-9. The Countess Rosmarin, whose château is on the Hungarian border, has friends on both sides; and gives shelter, without discrimination, to an Austrian deserter from the Hungarian army, and later—after the Hungarian defeat—to a Colonel of the Hungarian forces.

The Countess has a policy which one of her friends describes as 'divine non-interference', remarking at the same time that

> Lives make and unmake themselves in her neighbourhood.

When this policy—which seems to be no more than one of infinite attentive courtesy—is reduced by circumstances to its basic essentials, its constituents are seen to be: a respect for every person's individual uniqueness, and, springing from this, a belief in individual freedom of choice. She has, for example, many years ago, married her daughter to a *manqué* poet, Richard Gettner, who had already proved himself a waster; that is, in full knowledge of the probable results, she had let her daughter take her own misguided way without trying to influence her. The marriage, which remained unconsummated, rapidly broke down; and soon after, her daughter, Gelda, is remarried to Count Peter Zichy. At the start of the revolution, Gettner the nihilist, carried away by enthusiasm, joins the Hungarian rebels; but after a while he loses interest, and deserts. The Hungarians, afraid that information he possesses may reach the Austrians, seek him persistently, and track him to the Countess's château. Aware of Gettner's instability, and the seeming total purposelessness of the man, the Countess refuses to surrender him, preferring that her house shall be ransacked rather than betray an individual to a fate he cannot embrace. During his sanctuary, Gettner attempts to make love to his ex-wife Gelda, almost alienating her present husband Count Peter from her. Against the persuasions of her friends, the Countess continues faithful to her charge, with a kind of quixotic loyalty which only finally bears fruit at her death. In a similar manner, she undertakes to hide Colonel Janik from his pursuers—the very man who had commandeered her house when she was protecting Gettner.

In one sense, the play can be described as a companion-piece to *A Sleep of Prisoners*. But here, the 'case for pacifism', which the festival play presented in tragic terms, is given a predominantly comedic expression. And with this comedic treatment, there enters a greater sophistication, a fuller complexity of discussion. *A Sleep of Prisoners* was partisan drama, with the viewpoint of the playwright directly audible, so to speak. But between Fry's attitude and its expression, in the words of Countess Rosmarin in this later play, a greater objective distance intervenes. The situation is complicated, too, by the arguments of Richard Gettner, who represents an egoistic and Falstaffian version of pacifism, as distinct from the altruistic pacifism of Countess Rosmarin.

The language of this play is less floral than that of the other comedies. The decorative descriptions of the outside world, so often rife in Fry's figures-of-speech, have very largely been replaced by a poetry of the inner life. This results in a number of statements about the nature of human existence, which have the force of a maxim by a sort of less cynical La Rochefoucauld. 'There we have no free-will', the Countess says of love,

> At the one place of experience
> Where we're most at mercy, and where
> The decision will alter us to the end of our days,
> Our destination is fixed;
> We're elected into love.

One way of putting this would be to say that Fry appears increasingly, in his drama, to be substituting a psychological definitive style for that of his earlier expansive florid method. The rhetoric here cuts nearer to the bone.

The author has termed this work 'A Winter Comedy', and the play begins with some talk of an early morning sleigh-ride through the snow. There are, though, it seems, other less overt reasons for the reference to the season. One is, perhaps, the new bareness of diction; another, the general grimness of the plot, with its background of the miseries of war; and a third, maybe, the notion that this is a play fitted to the present time, the present apocalyptic age which, for all we know, might see 'the end of history', as the history of man so far has been enacted.

A comedy, it cannot too often be stressed—according to an ancient definition—is a play which ends happily; the nature of its resolution, and not the omnipresence of humour, being the essence of this species of drama. Now all of Fry's 'comedies of seasons' may be said to end happily, emotionally or spiritually—but only just. Happiness achieved by the skin of one's teeth might almost appear to be Fry's own personal understanding of comedy, in terms both of man's mortality and the special doom-conscious climate of our age.

The fourth of Fry's seasonal comedies—*A Yard of Sun* set in the immediate post-war Siena of July 1946—ends with an extravagant self-mocking gesture of acquiescence, as if a man should be both amused and amazed at himself: at his human nature, identity and fate. The subtle spirit of resignation—effectively demonstrative, theatrically speaking—with which the play closes, can be suggested to some degree by the stage directions before the curtain falls. The character Alfio has just, for the second time, avoided sudden death on his motorcycle.

(ALFIO grins, and gives the extravagant Neapolitan gesture he gave before, but this time ironically.
CESARE makes the same gesture in sympathetic reply. The others are laughing.)

There is a new note of inconsequentiality—the acceptance of something so absurd that laughter, or this humorous half-cavalier dismissal of things, appears man's only fit response. The close of *Venus Observed* clearly echoed Shakespeare's words 'the rest is silence'. Here, in *A Yard of Sun*, Fry's ultimate comment varies that phrase: the rest is laughter—a laughter, outwardly hilarious, perhaps, but containing a possible undertone of ultimate helplessness and defeat.

I have approached this fourth comedy back-to-front because certain commentators have failed to locate a serious expression of meaning within it. Those overburdened critics who cannot take time to peruse the whole play may, at this point, conveniently note that the essence or message is to be found in Act II on pages 103-4. Other readers will doubtless be content to approach the upshot in the more customary manner.

Set in July, the traditional month of the first Palio or ceremonial bare-backed horse race between the parishes of the city of Siena, *A Yard of Sun* completes Fry's seasonal quartet and is subtitled by him 'A Summer Comedy'. Strong as the atmospheric element in this drama is, the tie between season, characters and events does not appear to me so potent as in the other three comedies. In, for example, *Venus Observed* and *The Light is Dark Enough*, the seasonal element—as well as being markedly present in passages describing the natural scene—was also active in helping to create a sense of something analogous to Shakespeare's 'ages of man'. The Duke, for instance, in *Venus Observed* had arrived at that inner autumn of the emotions: a debonair but darkling middle-age. The coward and cynic Gettner in *The Dark is Light Enough* may likewise be thought to personify winter, not through any ageing process as in the Duke, but by reason of the psychological zero which his frozen egoism may be seen to represent.

Here, however, in *A Yard of Sun* the seasonal element of summer is to be envisaged as more widely diffused and not focused, as in the other plays, so concentratedly in one character. Another feature in this play is that the summer element seems to be interpreted in a number of diverse ways. It is reflected in both the *heat* of the streets of Siena, in the gathering *hot* spirit of struggle between the contenders and their fans concerning the coming Palio, and in the *heated* arguments among the members of the Bruno family recently reassembled after years of war. Summer is symbolized, too, in the warmth of amorous feelings, and in one long speech in particular in which Ana-Clara compares the ritual and contest of the Palio to 'an unhurried lovemaking', terminating 'when the corporate body has been tautened/ Absolutely to expectation's limit' in 'the violent release/The orgasm'. In addition, one may conjecture whether the title of the play itself does not hold a symbolical pun. *A Yard of Sun* is, in fact, a reference to a small stretch of street in Siena. Equally, however, it may point to the short space which man occupies on earth and the brief duration of his tenancy. One can—perhaps fancifully—read into the title some of the implications of Tolstoy's grim story *How Much Land does a Man Need?*—enough to bury him—and in that famous passage from Hobbes concerning the life of man:'solitary, poor, nasty, brutish, and short'. 'A yard', likewise, is but a little space; but 'A Yard of Sun' possibly suggests that the small measure of our existence is not without its beauty and glory, and warmth—even if that warmth includes the warmth of anger, division and violence.

The play, we can say, is about the prospects of reconciliation, hope and harmony for humanity as a whole. The specific time and place, however, is Siena in the immediate post-war; and the general import of the play is therefore stated in terms of one localized situation. People are returning from the war—from the Forces, prison-camps, hospitals and other places—and trying to pick up life anew. There is excitement in the air; and the age-old ceremony of the Palio, which acts as centre for this excitement, can be regarded as symbolizing the Phoenix urge or capacity in man. As the not-unsympathetic ex-Fascist character Luigi puts it:

> The week of the Palio—the sensational week,
> When the city celebrates an immortal identity,
> When it hymns our power of survival over oppression,
> Defeat and death.

For Luigi, the good life will return with the peace:

> The happy times are coming out of their shelter.
> They'll be a bit pale at first until the light
> Gets to the skin; but there's a taste in the air
> Of what it was like when we were boys . . .

At the same time, this feeling of resurgence has to meet the suspicion and hatred existing as a residue of the war. Fry's notion of the situation in this drama is powerfully enforced by a passage printed as epigraph in the programme to the play as first performed by the Nottingham Playhouse Company on 11 July 1970. It is taken from a book entitled *The Truce: A Survivor's Journey Home from Auschwitz* by Primo Levi (translated by Stuart Woolf, 1965):

What should we find at home? How much of ourselves had been eroded, extinguished? Were we returning richer or poorer, stronger or emptier? We did not know; but we knew that on the thresholds of our homes, for good or ill, a trial awaited us, and we anticipated it with fear... Soon, tomorrow, we should have to give battle, against enemies still unknown, outside ourselves and inside; with what weapons, what energies, what willpower?

In the family of Angelino Bruno, one son (a partisan) is now a doctor in general practice and a social revolutionary; another, Luigi (once a member of Mussolini's Blackshirts) today earns his living by 'reporting football matches in the local papers./As though they were grand opera', while the third, Edmondo, the black sheep of the family, renounced by his father before the war, now turns up as a millionaire, having lived in Portugal as a profiteer during the dark years, selling ores and commodities to all sides. Edmondo's plan is to put his 'bunkered family back on the fairway'—a project to advance his own egoism rather than one dictated by filial-fraternal feeling. Edmondo's rehabilitation plan does not receive unqualified support. The brothers quarrel; Edmondo departs; and it is left to the married lover of the Bruno's neighbour Giosetta Scapare to call for a new spirit in living. He, Cesare, has just returned, weary and tattered from a prisoner-of-war camp in Russia; and Roberto's plea for political revolution appears to him as a regressive act leading only to violence and further chaos. For Cesare, man's hope lies not in sudden overthrow of the Establish-

ment, but in internal metamorphosis—'the real revolution/
The transformation'.

Cesare's memories of the prison-camp, its filth and
cruelty, make him sceptical of violence as the way forward
to utopia:

> Don't, for God's sake, reward us
> By staring so long at the gorgon's head
> It grips the muscles of your living face.
> We've been in the dirt. We don't want to be remembered
> By generations playing at mud-pies
> And calling it the true image of life—
> I'd rather come soon to the clean skull.

There are references in this passage—over and above the
plot's situation—to various schools of materialistic thought,
and to a naïve contemporary materialism's very own
theatre: the Kitchen Sink.

Speech-wise, Fry is back, in this play, at some of his old
tricks. Imagery and rhetoric come tumbling forth in fuller,
less inhibited fashion than in *The Dark is Light Enough* (1954)
and *Curtmantle* (1961), his two immediately previous
productions. However grim or grey the experience referred
to in the play, the language retains its gaiety. Even so, the
style of *A Yard of Sun* is more colloquial and idiomatic than
that of his earlier comedies, which are consciously floral
and high-flown; and it is in this homelier weave that Fry
works the pattern of his figurative expressions. The same
increasing employment of, and variation on, proverbial
home-grown turns of speech is to be found in Fry's fine
version of Ibsen's *Peer Gynt* produced and published the
same year.

But if animation or gaiety of language is somehow
retained whatever the experience spoken of, the underlying
mood or tone of the play is quite another matter. A qualified
pessimism, lit at frequent intervals by the summer lightning
of optimism might serve as an approximate description.
Fry obviously approaches his theme with goodwill to man-

kind and a certain hope, but these go severely burdened by grave doubts as to our powers of self-preservation and revival.

(c) *Tragedy*

Tragedy is distinguished from comedy by its greater degree of inevitability: when the course of Falstaff's[1] life is seen as inevitable, he ceases to be a comic character and becomes imbued with a deep pathos. It is, then, the more powerful current of inevitability which we feel flowing through Fry's tragedy *The Firstborn* that sets it apart from his comedies.

The play is based on the captivity of the Jews under the Pharaoh, and of their escape subsequent to the Seven Plagues. Moses intercedes with God for the freedom of the Israelites, but finds, when this freedom is obtained, that it entails the sacrifice of Rameses (at the hands of the Angel of Death), son of the Pharaoh, and his own nephew-by-adoption. Fry has admitted[2] that he is guilty of an insufficient emphasis of meaning in this climax; for many of the critics felt that Moses' despair at the realization that victory would be accomplished only at the cost of Rameses' death had not been adequately prepared for; since Moses' affection for his nephew had not been strongly stressed in the preceding scenes. 'Now', writes Fry, 'I had not imagined any such personal affection on the part of Moses. In the play he meets Rameses for a bare five minutes: is touched by his hero-worship: recognizes the boy's sincerity and humanity, and that is all. What I hoped I had shown, and hadn't, was that to Moses the boy represented Moses' own boyhood when he was Prince of Egypt, represented also that love for Egypt which Moses couldn't shake off even when he was fighting her. There are certainly speeches to that effect, and Moses in the moment of realization, cries 'Egypt, Egypt! He was meant for Egypt!'; but the speeches were not enough.'

[1] See Shakespeare's *Henry IV*, Parts I and II.
[2] See *An Experience of Critics* (1952).

I have thought it right to instance this point, as it serves to express the playwright's partial dissatisfaction with the play; but to me it does not seem a substantial error. In either case (sympathy for or love of the young Prince as an individual *or* as heir-apparent—representing Egypt), the necessity, the sacrifice, and the sense of loss remain. The tragic denouement is in no wise interrupted.

The Firstborn is Fry's most exalted work. It is a moving study of the anguish and ecstasy of a dedicated man; of one whose natural hopes and fears are smothered (being put to a painful emotional death), in the service of a self-tran-scendent ideal. As Moses says to Rameses, who pleads on behalf of his country smitten with the Plagues:

> You appeal to Moses,
> But Moses is now only a name and an obedience.
> It is the God of the Hebrews, springing out
> Of unknown ambush, a vigour moving
> In a great shadow, who draws the bow
> Of his mystery, to loose this punishing arrow
> Feathered with my face; he who in his hour
> Broke the irreparable dam which kept his thought,
> Released the cataract birth and death
> To storm across time and the world;
> He who in his morning
> Drew open the furious petals of the sun;
> He who through his iron fingers
> Lets all go, lets all waste and go,
> Except, dearly retained in his palm, the soul.

In no other play by Fry are the characters so securely depicted. The people in this drama do not dwell in the single dimension of 'stage' time. We learn of their pasts, and how their pasts exist like open wounds informing their present: Anath's undying obsession with Moses; Miriam's bitter fear for her son Shendi, bred from experience of old conspiracies; the Pharaoh's exhaustion in the cause of Egypt, with its private history of sleepless nights; and Teusret's identification with her brother Rameses, and her desolation at the thought of his marriage. We can peer down the words of all these characters into their bygone years which have made them what they are.

In *The Firstborn* we are presented with a debate between tyranny and self-responsibility. Freedom wins the day, but only at a price. Human action seldom offers us the chance of endless possibilities or the compulsion of a single necessity. Our existence is a dialectic of the two, a condition which *The Firstborn* brilliantly demonstrates.

(d) *Fry, Anouilh, Giraudoux, and Ibsen*

Fry has made five translations from the French playwrights Jean Anouilh and Jean Giraudoux. In 1950, he published *Ring round the Moon*, a partly changed version of the former's *L'Invitation au Château*. This was followed, in 1955, by *The Lark*, a rendition of Anouilh's *L'Alouette*, and *Tiger at the Gates*, the English title Fry has chosen for Giraudoux's *La Guerre de Troie n'aura pas lieu*. Two further translations from Giraudoux were *Duel of Angels* (from *Pour Lucrèce*) in 1958 and *Judith* in 1959.

The first of these plays was a social comedy, described as 'A Charade with Music', and on its appearance led to the comparison of Anouilh and Fry as like-minded playwrights. This, perhaps, was a little beside the point. Anouilh has more wit but less humour, greater lightness but less depth of meaning, is perter but less poetic, than Fry. On the other hand, both are born 'theatricians', men who delight to utilize with skill the limited floor-space of stage convention. It may therefore be truer to say that though these two hold a different drama in mind, Fry appreciates Anouilh for the buoyant mastery of his medium.

The Lark and *Tiger at the Gates* share an important purpose in common. Both of them colloquialize, in a modern fashion, the treatment of a grand or heroic subject; the first the story of Joan of Arc, the second, that of the tale of Troy.

In this, we find a parallel with Fry's own work; for in *The Lady's Not for Burning*, he has treated a medieval theme without a trace of archaic stiffness and with a fresh suppleness of speech which a plot from the past often kills off in a poet.[1]

The Lark, Tiger at the Gates, Duel of Angels and *Judith* scale down the giant denizens of myth to the measurements of living men and women. This is not the same as debunking them, but consists rather in a process of 'naturalizing' them in the human sphere. For Fry, Anouilh, and Giraudoux, the heroes and demi-gods of legend are, in the end, fellow mortals, however marvellous such mortals may be.[2]

Fry's translations, up to this point, are significant, too, for another reason. They represent the poet submitting himself to the Lenten discipline of prose (which, for the writer of verse, can seem a hard sentence). But there is every cause to believe that Fry, though conscientious in this matter, was enjoying his penance hugely. Conductor of the full orchestra of words, as his poetic dramas prove him to be, he comes before us in these translations as a pianist of honest and agile distinction, an executant artist besides a rare composer.

Perhaps, though, it is only when the adaptation made by him constitutes a challenge represented by a masterpiece of the first order that we see what his powers really are in this direction. Such a drama was the English version which he made in 1970 of Ibsen's five-act play *Peer Gynt*. Fry, here, based his work on a literal translation by Johan Fillinger. The play was performed as the opening item in the Chichester Festival of that year; and, following paperback publication, takes its place as Volume III of the Oxford Ibsen, under the general editorship of Professor James Walter McFarlane.

---

[1] The natural behaviour and easy fun of *The Boy with a Cart* and *Thor, with Angels* show Fry attempting a similar thing in the somewhat starched world of religious drama.

[2] What these playwrights are tilting at is not the recognition of mystery but exegesis according to the 'text-book' sublime. See, in this connexion, Anouilh's Programme Note to the first French performance of *L'Alouette*, reprinted on the dust-cover of Fry's translation *The Lark*.

However one regards Ibsen's great national extravaganza, in which realism and fantasy alternate and meet, the advanced experimental aspect of its form simply cannot be gainsaid. An episodic picaresque construction provides the general build of the play; and part of any adapter's business is to catch the drama's brisk pace (expressed in the pell-mell horse-play of its action) while not losing Ibsen's reflective turn of thought which so unexpectedly mingles with, or off-sets, the almost slap-stick exuberance.

This is exactly what Fry has achieved; and we can well understand how the indefinable mixed genre of this play would appeal to him as possessing certain of his own notions. 'Comedy', writes Fry, 'is an escape, not from truth but from despair.' 'A narrow escape,' he adds. Another element we discover in Ibsen (along with a dung-like earthiness of humour) is frank sentimentality—we need only think of Aase's death scene—a quality openly evident in Fry, for which one or two sensitive critics (sensitive, that is, to the fashion for the tough) have manfully rebuked him.

In adapting Ibsen into English, Fry had two main contestants to consider: William Archer, whose translation appeared in 1907, and R. Ellis Roberts, whose version followed just five years later. Archer admitted that what he sought to manufacture was a crib to *Peer Gynt*, 'a faithful transcript'. Ellis Roberts, on the other hand, confessed to higher ambitions: a rendering which should provide something of the 'luxuriant complexity of rhyme and metre' which characterizes the original. Fry clearly concentrated on what Archer took to be the predominant trait of Ibsen's language: 'its vernacular ease and simplicity'.

'My book *is* poetry,' Ibsen insisted, infuriated by fancy reviewers, and it is just this poetry (a compound of homely diction and dynamic colloquialism) which Fry has brought out fully for the first time. The greater ease and naturalism of his version can be readily assessed when one compares the way he renders Aase's first longish speech with R. Ellis Robert's translation. Here is the latter's:

> How can you face your mother? You—!
> Just when work is worst, you rush
> Off to hunt thro' snow and slush;
> Then with your clothes in rags and tatters
> Home you come; and what more matters,
> Lose your gun and kill no game:
> And with round and innocent eyes
> Want me to believe your lame
> Catalogue of hunters' lies!

and here is Fry's:

> Would you even try and cheat your mother?
> First you slope off into the mountains
> For weeks when we're busy haymaking
> And go chasing reindeer over the snow;
> Then you come home, a mass of scratches,
> Without your gun or as much as a rabbit;
> And now you stare me in the face
> And think I'll believe this stuff about *hunting*!

Fry's version has the sound of spoken speech—excited language used by an indignant women. It is lively with idiomatic phrases and expressions: 'slope off,' 'go chasing,' 'a mass of scratches'. In contrast to this Ellis Roberts' is still *written or literary speech*. Compare his locution 'with round and innocent eyes' with Fry's colloquial 'stare me in the face'.

In order to give himself fuller scope for this simulacrum of naturalness, Fry dispenses with rhyme which Ibsen himself employed. In a letter to me he remarked that he had 'experimented for a day or two with the possibility of rhyme—but it would have to have strayed further from Ibsen's words; and it would have sounded like Mother Goose'.

With regard to the rhythm of the original, Fry told me in the same letter that he had 'tried to keep very close to Ibsen's metrical scheme: the four-foot line where he uses it (though perhaps a bit more freely than he does)—changing to the three-foot line for the "One castle piled on another" speech, and the death of Aase, etc. and the blank verse line for the graveside speech, as he does'.

William Archer, in the Introduction to his own pioneer rendering of *Peer Gynt*, had followed a course similar to Fry's, namely 'a translation as nearly as possible in the metres of the original, but with the rhymes suppressed'. Where Fry was to prove superior to Archer was in his finer sense of diction. His version can claim to be the first English triumph in avoiding the substitution of conventional poetic phrasing and padding for the racy terseness of Ibsen's 'living language' poem.

(e) *A History Play*

For seven years—since *The Dark is Light Enough*—Fry wrote no fresh play of his own. He spent the time script-writing in Rome for such epic 'productions' as the film *Ben Hur*, and incubating his long-awaited drama on Henry II. In 1961 the text of the work was published under the title of *Curtmantle* (a reference to the short unpretentious coat which the otherwise kingly monarch wore).

The structure of *Curtmantle* is curious. It bears some resemblance to Shakespeare's chronicle plays, and it is just possible that the panoramic sweep of historical films has had some influence on its unfolding. But the purpose behind the composition is defined for us in Fry's own words: 'the form it takes is one of memory and contemplation', just as *A Sleep of Prisoners* found a form to represent the process of dreaming.

Henry II's career as a vigorous king, to the time of his defeat and death, is presented, with no Joycean trimmings,[1] through the memory of Marshal, an old man who once served him. It is, in this sense, that *Curtmantle* is not an historical narrative purely. The light is not so evenly distri-

---

[1] The inner monologue, and flow of consciousness, have no part in shaping this play.

buted on the characters as in some of Shakespeare's histories. It is the Muse of Biography seeking to uncover the essence of the King—'simple and royal . . . direct and paradoxical, compassionate and hard, a man of intellect, a man of action, God-fearing, superstitious, blasphemous, far-seeing, short-sighted, affectionate, lustful, patient, volcanic, humble, and overriding'—whose operations we watch in this play.

Curtmantle is also a curious play in that it does not provide the King with a main antagonist. Becket is only one opponent. There are others: the barons, his sons, and his Queen. Henry's chief enemy is himself: he plans and builds beyond his reach. Time steals his vigour, and his plans collapse about him. His ambitions destroy him like the crash of falling columns.

As in his early piece *The Boy with a Cart*, Fry has used both prose and verse. The poetry has lost its puppy-fat; and, if never studiously flat or urbane after the manner of *The Cocktail Party*, it is grim with the iron of argument. Invective can still light up the lines with a wild glare as of fire in some of the King's angry speeches, but Fry's 'kingfisher' style is absent. The verse is as stern as the feathers of an eagle.

To many this play may have proved a disappointment. The tinsel-and-Chinese lantern world of the Comedies is left behind, and we are back to the theme of power which dominated Fry's tragedy *The Firstborn*. The problem of authority—how to exercise it, and yet remain human; how to serve the State, yet still cherish the individual—these are the predicaments which Henry II shares with the Pharoah.

But whereas in *The Firstborn*, we are shown the Pharoah as a man with no private life left undevoured by matters of state, in *Curtmantle* the King is presented as more than a wielder of power. We see the man, with all his dilemmas, as a 'many-souled'[1] personality. Perhaps Henry remains an enigma, but the life of that enigma is felt throughout the play.

With the King we have Archbishop Becket. That goes

[1] Not Fry's, but Jack Kerouac's, phrase.

without saying. But the hagiographical imagination, for all Fry's 'reverence for life,' is not active here. As Marshal, the King's servant, says of Thomas, as person and prelate, in retrospective:

> he seemed to me like a man
> Who has gone through life saving up all passion
> To spend at last on his own downfall.

'Don't be too proud to live,' the King had once counselled him; and in Act III we hear no more of Becket, other matters of moment occupying the stage.

Some critics have held this against the playwright; but Fry presents the Saint as of limited interest beside the many-faceted King. The mystery of the monarch is a deeper affair just as his tragedy is less single-minded. Then, too, at the start of his play, Fry sets his action earlier than Eliot. In *Murder in the Cathedral*, Thomas is already Archbishop. The road to martyrdom cannot be avoided without, as he sees it, betraying the Church. But in *Curtmantle*, Thomas is free to reject the offer of the Primacy, feeling as he does the dissension which it must breed between him and the King (and knowing, too, one would have thought as the King's companion and adviser, how Henry would view his actions as treachery).

That Fry, with his religious imagination, should none the less invest the play with a subtle but discernible secular bias is a mark of his sensitive independence. Osborne, in *Luther*, re-enacts history in the light of Marx: Eliot spies upon it through a stained-glass window. It is hard to view it simply through the eyes of one's own mind.

IV. SUMMARY

The mainspring of Fry's work is his intuition of the presence of mystery. For him, this element is not located somewhere inviolably aloof or aloft like Plato's realm of

Pure Ideas, but is something continually informing our mortality. As Moses tells his brother in *The Firstborn*:

> Creation's mutehead is dissolving, Aaron.
> Our lives are being lived into our lives.

This sense, which Fry possesses, of one dimension of meaning lurking behind another, makes him sceptical of any cut-and-dried logical scheme. The universe has not been docketed and filed as completely as we sometimes incline to believe. So Aaron, the matter-of-fact soldier, under the influence of Moses' vision, remarks, in the same play:

> I've begun to believe the reasonable
> Is an invention of man, altogether in opposition
> To the facts of creation.

Man's last words, when confronted with existence, are Peter's in *A Sleep of Prisoners*:

> Deal me high, deal me low.
> Make my deeds
> My nameless needs.
> I know I do not know.

The fourth line might be read as an agnostic confession; but it is an agnosticism so brimful of religious wonder, of the feel of the numinous, that to class it under the heading of the more scientific Victorian free-thought would obviously be an error. One of Fry's chief endeavours, I feel, is to keep open the door upon the fourth dimension. Definition of any sort, whether religious or materialistic, seems to him to close that door; for, as he somewhere observes, 'a spade is never merely a spade'.

It is not only in the trafficking between time and eternity, between the natural and the supernatural (to make use of these hard-and-fast categories) that Fry finds the process of mystery. He discovers it, too, in the thoughts behind a thought, in 'the other meaning' at the back of a statement, that we are often aware of in intercourse. Ambiguity, to him, represents a rich field for poetical and psychological exploration.

But the ambiguity encountered in Fry differs from the erudite mystification which certain members of the modern school favour. The ambiguity Fry practises does not depend for its interpretation upon literary or classical allusions.[1] In this sense, it is not a poetry of culture and knowledge, but one which seeks to represent the natural workings of the mind. All those transitions by means of which one thought passes to another thought (behind which it was hiding, so to speak) at the promptings of verbal association are of particular interest to Fry, and have yielded him a full poetical return.

I have already instanced Fry's use of the *double entendre*; and it is important perhaps to stress again that the second meaning which the words conceal is often perpetrated by a character only half-aware of it, or quite unaware, or beginning to be aware. One of the best illustrations of this occurs in *A Phoenix Too Frequent*, where Tegeus and Dynamene, caught in the whirlpool of their passion for each other are, rapidly drawing to its centre, trying to withhold a mutual declaration by desperately talking about impersonal things. The passage (beginning 'Tell me, What is your opinion of Progress . . .'), with its sexual image of the concertina as a figure for human evolution, is full of implications on several levels. Bawdy, which is present in plenty in this play, is unmistakable, but wears lace-gloves.

Stemming, likewise, from Fry's feeling for mystery is the *baptismal* quality in many of his phrases. The words immerse his subject in a dimension which gives to them a new or added significance. How much of the puzzle of birth and

---

[1] For example, Tegeus' 'oath-speech' ('I swear by Horkos and the Styx . . .') does not depend, for appreciation, upon a knowledge of the proper names mentioned. It is a piece of 'pure poetry', of pure fantasy employed for humorous effect.

existence is suggested in this speech by David in *A Sleep of Prisoners*!

> I was trusted
> Into breath. Why am I doubted now?
> Flesh is my birthplace.

Fry's unusual power over words frequently lends itself to virtuosity.[1] If this end does not conflict with the dramatic tempo and situation (as I feel it does in Perpetua's monologue, Act II, scene ii, in *Venus Observed*, beginning 'There isn't any reason . . .'), it provides us, especially in the comedies, with a buoyancy of entertainment the more relieving through its contrast to the 'dead-pan' diction of our recent stage. But there is a tendency in Fry to allow this ebullience to run into *longueurs*. '*Sufflaminandus erat*'—as Ben Jonson observed of a great contemporary. Fry needs the brakes applied from time to time;[2] but one of our chief pleasures in this playwright must be in his splendid use of the full-throttle. There is no lack of horse-power[3] in his talent.

---

[1] In writing on Milton, T. S. Eliot has remarked that 'an enjoyment by the author in the exercise of his own virtuosity' is 'a mark of the first rank of genius'.

[2] The language of *A Sleep of Prisoners*, Fry's last religious play, rather suggests that he has been giving some attention to this. While remaining as vivid as that of the comedies, it is a good deal starker and controlled (by the import of the dramatic moment).

[3] Fry constitutes something of an exception to what we may term the neo-classical Self-denying Ordinance, which Roy Campbell so cogently parodied:

> You praise the firm restraint with which they write—
>   I'm with you there, of course:
> They use the snaffle and the curb all right
>   But where's the bloody horse!

CHRISTOPHER FRY

A Bibliography

(Place of publication London, unless stated otherwise)

Bibliography:
'A Bibliography on Christopher Fry', compiled by B. L. Schear and
E. G. Prater, *Tulane Drama Review*, Vol IV, iii, March 1960,
88–98.

Collected Works
THREE PLAYS: The Firstborn; Thor, with Angels; A Sleep of Prisoners
(1960).
PLAYS (1969)
—contains *A Phoenix too Frequent; Thor, with Angels; The Lady's not
for Burning.*

Separate Works
THE BOY WITH A CART: Cuthman, Saint of Sussex: A Play (1939).
A PHOENIX TOO FREQUENT: A Comedy (1946).
THE FIRSTBORN: A Play in three Acts; Cambridge (1946)
—revised 1958.
THE LADY'S NOT FOR BURNING: A Comedy (1949).
THOR, WITH ANGELS: A Play (1950).
VENUS OBSERVED: A Play (1950).
A SLEEP OF PRISONERS: A Play (1951).
AN EXPERIENCE OF CRITICS, ed. K. Webb (1952). *Criticism*
THE DARK IS LIGHT ENOUGH (1954). *Drama*
CURTMANTLE: A Play (1961).
A YARD OF SUN: A Comedy (1970).

Translations:
RING ROUND THE MOON (1950). *Charade with music*
—a translation of *L'Invitation au Château*, by J. Anouilh. Acting
edition, 1952.
THE LARK (1955)
—a translation of *L'Alouette*, by J. Anouilh.
TIGER AT THE GATES (1955)
—a translation of *La Guerre de Troie n'aura pas lieu*, by J. Giraudoux.

49

DUEL OF ANGELS (1958)
—a translation of *Pour Lucrèce*, by J. Giraudoux.
JUDITH (1959)
—translated from *Judith*, by J. Giraudoux.
THE BOY AND THE MAGIC (1964). *A Tale*
—a translation of *L'Enfant et les sortilèges*, by Colette.
PEER GYNT (1970)
—based on a literal translation of Ibsen's *Peer Gynt* by J. Fillinger.

Some Biographical and Critical Studies:
CHRISTOPHER FRY: An Appreciation, by D. Stanford (1951)
—in a revised edition of this work, published in 1952, a chapter on *A Sleep of Prisoners* replaces one on 'Critics and Criticism'.
CHRISTOPHER FRY ALBUM, ed. D. Stanford (1952).
DRAMA FROM IBSEN TO ELIOT, by R. Williams (1952)
—includes a section on Christopher Fry in a chapter entitled 'Some Verse Dramatists'.
DRAMATISTS OF TODAY, by J. C. Trewin (1953)
—includes a chapter on Fry entitled 'A Man of his Word'.
CHRISTOPHER FRY ET LA COMÉDIE DES SAISONS, by W. M. Merchant, P. de Rothschild, O. Mandel and M. Lebesque; Paris (1962)
—the title of 'Cahiers Renaud-Barrault'. No. 39, which also includes an essay 'De la Comédie', by Christopher Fry and a translation of *A Phoenix too Frequent*.
STUDIEN ZUR DRAMATURGIE DES 'RELIGIOUS FESTIVAL PLAY' BEI CHRISTOPHER FRY, by H. Itschert; Tübingen (1963).
THE DRAMA OF COMEDY: Victim and Victor, by N. Vos; Richmond, Virginia (1966)
—includes a chapter dealing with Fry entitled 'The Comic Victim-Victor'.
LES PARADIS PERDUS: Essais critiques, by V. Dupont; Toulouse (1967)
—includes an essay 'Va-t-on brûler la sorcière'.
CHRISTOPHER FRY: The Man and his Works, by E. Roy (1969).

WRITERS AND THEIR WORK

BYRON: Bernard Blackstone
CARLYLE: David Gascoyne
LEWIS CARROLL: Derek Hudson
COLERIDGE: Kathleen Raine
CREEVEY & GREVILLE: J. Richardson
DE QUINCEY: Hugh Sykes Davies
DICKENS: K. J. Fielding
   EARLY NOVELS: T. Blount
   LATER NOVELS: B. Hardy
DISRAELI: Paul Bloomfield
GEORGE ELIOT: Lettice Cooper
FERRIER & GALT: W. M. Parker
FITZGERALD: Joanna Richardson
ELIZABETH GASKELL: Miriam Allott
GISSING: A. C. Ward
THOMAS HARDY: R. A. Scott-James
                    and C. Day Lewis
HAZLITT: J. B. Priestley
HOOD: Laurence Brander
G. M. HOPKINS: Geoffrey Grigson
T. H. HUXLEY: William Irvine
KEATS: Edmund Blunden
LAMB: Edmund Blunden
LANDOR: G. Rostrevor Hamilton
EDWARD LEAR: Joanna Richardson
MACAULAY: G. R. Potter
MEREDITH: Phyllis Bartlett
JOHN STUART MILL: M. Cranston
WILLIAM MORRIS: P. Henderson
NEWMAN: J. M. Cameron
PATER: Iain Fletcher
PEACOCK: J. I. M. Stewart
ROSSETTI: Oswald Doughty
CHRISTINA ROSSETTI: G. Battiscombe
RUSKIN: Peter Quennell
SIR WALTER SCOTT: Ian Jack
SHELLEY: G. M. Matthews
SOUTHEY: Geoffrey Carnall
LESLIE STEPHEN: Phyllis Grosskurth
R. L. STEVENSON: G. B. Stern
SWINBURNE: H. J. C. Grierson
TENNYSON: B. C. Southam
THACKERAY: Laurence Brander
FRANCIS THOMPSON: P. Butter
TROLLOPE: Hugh Sykes Davies
OSCAR WILDE: James Laver
WORDSWORTH: Helen Darbishire

Twentieth Century:
CHINUA ACHEBE: A. Ravenscroft
W. H. AUDEN: Richard Hoggart
HILAIRE BELLOC: Renée Haynes
ARNOLD BENNETT: F. Swinnerton
EDMUND BLUNDEN: Alec M. Hardie
ROBERT BRIDGES: J. Sparrow
ROY CAMPBELL: David Wright
JOYCE CARY: Walter Allen
G. K. CHESTERTON: C. Hollis

WINSTON CHURCHILL: John Connell
R. G. COLLINGWOOD: E. W. F. Tomlin
I. COMPTON-BURNETT:
                    R. Glynn Grylls
JOSEPH CONRAD: Oliver Warner
WALTER DE LA MARE: K. Hopkins
NORMAN DOUGLAS: Ian Greenlees
LAWRENCE DURRELL: G. S. Fraser
T. S. ELIOT: M. C. Bradbrook
FIRBANK & BETJEMAN: J. Brooke
FORD MADOX FORD: Kenneth Young
E. M. FORSTER: Rex Warner
CHRISTOPHER FRY: Derek Stanford
JOHN GALSWORTHY: R. H. Mottram
WM. GOLDING: Clive Pemberton
ROBERT GRAVES: M. Seymour-Smith
GRAHAM GREENE: Francis Wyndham
L. P. HARTLEY: Paul Bloomfield
A. E. HOUSMAN: Ian Scott-Kilvert
ALDOUS HUXLEY: Jocelyn Brooke
HENRY JAMES: Michael Swan
PAMELA HANSFORD JOHNSON:
                    Isabel Quigly
JAMES JOYCE: J. I. M. Stewart
RUDYARD KIPLING: Bonamy Dobrée
D. H. LAWRENCE: Kenneth Young
C. DAY LEWIS: Clifford Dyment
WYNDHAM LEWIS: E. W. F. Tomlin
COMPTON MACKENZIE: K. Young
LOUIS MACNEICE: John Press
KATHERINE MANSFIELD: Ian Gordon
JOHN MASEFIELD: L. A. G. Strong
SOMERSET MAUGHAM: J. Brophy
GEORGE MOORE: A. Norman Jeffares
J. MIDDLETON MURRY: Philip Mairet
SEAN O'CASEY: W. A. Armstrong
GEORGE ORWELL: Tom Hopkinson
JOHN OSBORNE: Simon Trussler
HAROLD PINTER: John Russell Taylor
POETS OF 1939–45 WAR: R. N. Currey
POWYS BROTHERS: R. C. Churchill
J. B. PRIESTLEY: Ivor Brown
HERBERT READ: Francis Berry
FOUR REALIST NOVELISTS: V. Brome
BERNARD SHAW: A. C. Ward
EDITH SITWELL: John Lehmann
KENNETH SLESSOR: C. Semmler
C. P. SNOW: William Cooper
SYNGE & LADY GREGORY: E. Coxhead
DYLAN THOMAS: G. S. Fraser
G. M. TREVELYAN: J. H. Plumb
WAR POETS: 1914–18: E. Blunden
EVELYN WAUGH: Christopher Hollis
H. G. WELLS: Montgomery Belgion
PATRICK WHITE: R. F. Brissenden
ANGUS WILSON: K. W. Gransden
VIRGINIA WOOLF: B. Blackstone
W. B. YEATS: G. S. Fraser